ABC AFFIRMATIONS

TO OUR YOUNG EMPERORS AND EMPRESSES

IAM4D

ISBN 978-93-5610-766-3
© IAM4D 2022
Published in India 2022 by Pencil

Contributors:
Co-Author: Tahirah Francis (mummy)
Co-Author: Tahirah Francis (mummy)
Editor: Donna Miller
Editor: Donna Miller

A brand of
One Point Six Technologies Pvt. Ltd.
123, Building J2, Shram Seva Premises,
Wadala Truck Terminal, Wadala (E)
Mumbai 400037, Maharashtra, INDIA
E connect@thepencilapp.com
W www.thepencilapp.com

Author biography

BY CHILDREN FOR CHILDREN

This book was written off the back of lock-down (COVID-19), to help with home learning mummy made us use affirmations to help us with phonics. once it became fun we asked mum if we could make a book to share with our friends when school opens up. so we worked super hard to created this book to share with everyone.

we choose the name IAM4D as its the letters mixed-up from our name

I is for Ishmaheel & Idris
A is for Aleena
M is for Malaika
4 for the 4 of US
D is for our family name Danmole

We hope you feel just as empowered as we do.

TEAM KNOW YOUR VALUE!

CONTENTS

Preface

To my young Emperors and Empresses

Always remember who you are

You have the potential to fullfil,

at everything you choose to do!

"YOU ARE EVERYTHING"

If there are any

words that you do not

understand.

Ask an adult to

Explain.

TEAM KNOW YOUR VALUE!

Acknowledgements

Euphemia Dedora Bloomfield
17/03/1943-14/12/2008

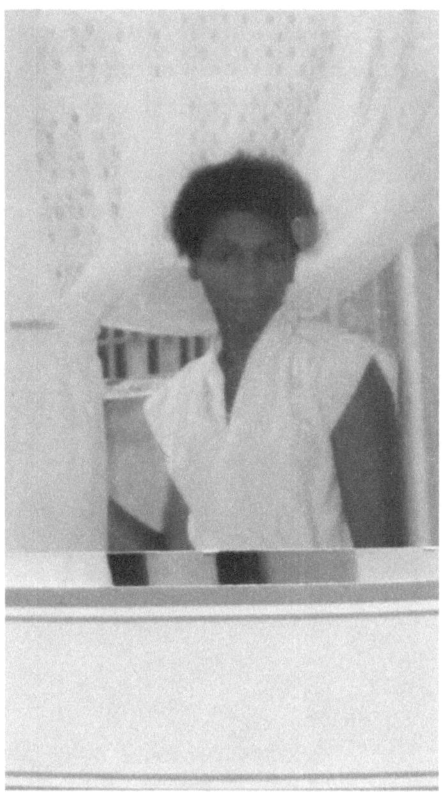

Our Rose From Rose Hill (JA) GRANDMA ROSE

Firstly we would like to send our thanks to "The Most High" for the abalities we have been gifted with....The power to achieve, believe and make our little dreams reality.

To Our **Great Grandma ROSE**the start of our Regal heritage, we rooted well.... We are so greatful to be choosen to have your royal DNA running through. **Grandma Qamara**thank you for all that you do, helping mummy shape us as leaders for the future. **Mummy**, you did it we are great example of you. **Daddy**thank you for being our king, to all our Danmole family thank you.

A special thank you to our editoral and inspirational team: **Donna Miller**, **Jonelle Dufus**, **Reva Felix**and **Trisha Ennis**we love you all and are ever so greatful for all that you do.

IT TAKES A VILLAGE TO RAISE A CHILD, WE ARE PROUD TO BE VILLAGE CHILDREN

A

A

Reader says..... YOU ARE	NOW YOU SAY
AFRICAN	I AM AFRICAN
AMAZING	I AM AMAZING
AMBITIOUS	I AM AMBITIOUS
ATHLETIC	I AM ATHLETIC

HOW DO YOU FEEL?

ALEENA

Aleena

I AM A STAR,

I WILL ALWAYS SHINE

SO BRIGHTLY,

I AM AN AMAZING PERSON!

I HAVE THE POTENTIAL

TO FULLFIL

AT EVERYTHING

I CHOOSE TO DO……

ALEENA DANMOLE

B

B

Reader says..... YOU ARE	NOW YOU SAY
BLACK	I AM BLACK
BEAUTIFUL	I AM BEAUTIFUL
BLESSED	I AM BLESSED
BRILLIANT	I AM BRILLIANT

HOW DO YOU FEEL?

C

C

Reader says..... YOU ARE	NOW YOU SAY
CULTURED	I AM CULTURED
CONFIDENT	I AM CONFIDENT
CHOSEN	I AM CHOSEN
CLEVER	I AM CLEVER

HOW DO YOU FEEL?

D

D

Reader says..... YOU ARE	NOW YOU SAY
DIGNIFIED	I AM DIGNIFIED
DESERVING	I AM DESERVING
DESTINED	I AM DESTINED
DELIGHTFUL	I AM DELIGHTFUL

HOW DO YOU FEEL?

E

E

Reader says..... YOU ARE	NOW YOU SAY
EDUCATED	I AM EDUCATED
EMPOWERED	I AM EMPOWERED
EXCELLENT	I AM EXCELLENT
EQUAL	I AM EQUAL

HOW DO YOU FEEL?

F

F

Reader says..... YOU ARE	NOW YOU SAY
FREE	I AM FREE
FOCUSED	I AM FOCUSED
FANTASTIC	I AM FANTASTIC
FEARLESS	I AM FEARLESS

HOW DO YOU FEEL?

G

G

Reader says..... YOU ARE	NOW YOU SAY
GREAT	I AM GREAT
GENIUS	I AM GENIUS
GODLY	I AM GODLY
GENUINE	I AM GENUINE

HOW DO YOU FEEL?

H

H

Reader says..... YOU ARE	NOW YOU SAY
HISTORIC	I AM HISTORIC
HONOURABLE	I AM HONOURABLE
HELPFUL	I AM HELPFUL
HEROIC	I AM HEROIC

HOW DO YOU FEEL?

ISHMAHEEL

Ishmaheel

I AM A KING,

IT'S DESIGNED

IN MY

DNA TO WIN,

I AM DETERMINED!

I HAVE THE POTENIAL

TO FULLFIL

AT EVERYTHING

I CHOOSE TO DO....

ISHMAHEEL DANMOLE

I

I

Reader says..... YOU ARE	NOW YOU SAY
INTELLIGENT	I AM INTELLIGENT
IMPORTANT	I AM IMPORTANT
INFLUENTIAL	I AM INFLUENTIAL
INSPIRATIONAL	I AM INSPIRATIONAL

HOW DO YOU FEEL?

IDRIS

Idris

I AM AN EMPEROR,

I AM

HERE TO BUILD

AN EMPIRE,

I AM A SURVIVOR!

I HAVE THE POTENTIAL

TO FULLFIL

AT EVERYTHING

I CHOOSE TO DO….

IDRIS DANMOLE

J

J

Reader says..... YOU ARE	NOW YOU SAY
JOYFUL	I AM JOYFUL
JOLLY	I AM JOLLY
JUSTIFIED	I AM JUSTIFIED
JAZZY	I AM JAZZY

HOW DO YOU FEEL?

K

K

Reader says..... YOU ARE	NOW YOU SAY
KNOWING	I AM KNOWING
KNOWLEDGE	I AM KNOWLEDGE
KIND	I AM KIND
KNIGHTLY	I AM KNIGHTLY

HOW DO YOU FEEL?

L

L

Reader says..... YOU ARE	NOW YOU SAY
LOVED	I AM LOVED
LEGENDARY	I AM LEGENDARY
LIMITLESS	I AM LIMITLESS
LOVABLE	I AM LOVABLE

HOW DO YOU FEEL?

M

M

Reader says..... YOU ARE	NOW YOU SAY
MAJESTIC	I AM MAJESTIC
MARVELOUS	I AM MARVELOUS
MAGNIFICENT	I AM MAGNIFICENT
MAJOR	I AM MAJOR

HOW DO YOU FEEL?

MALAIKA

Malaika

I AM a diamond,

So delicate and precious,

I have

a strength

like no other,

I have the potential

to fullfil

at everything

I choose to do...

MALAIKA DANMOLE

N

N

Reader says..... YOU ARE	NOW YOU SAY
NATURED	I AM NATURED
NOBLE	I AM NOBLE
NEEDED	I AM NEEDED
NICE	I AM NICE

HOW DO YOU FEEL?

O

o

Reader says..... YOU ARE	NOW YOU SAY
ORGANISED	I AM ORGANISED
OUTSTANDING	I AM OUTSTANDING
ORIGINAL	I AM ORIGINAL
ONE	I AM ONE

HOW DO YOU FEEL?

P

P

Reader says..... YOU ARE	NOW YOU SAY
PROUD	I AM PROUD
POWERFUL	I AM POWERFUL
PERSISTANT	I AM PERSISTANT
PHENOMINAL	I AM PHENOMINAL

HOW DO YOU FEEL?

Q

Q

Reader says..... YOU ARE	NOW YOU SAY
QUALITY	I AM QUALITY
QUANTITY	I AM QUANTITY
QUICK-THINKING	I AM QUICK-THINKING
QUALIFIED	I AM QUALIFIED

HOW DO YOU FEEL?

R

R

Reader says..... YOU ARE	NOW YOU SAY
ROOTED	I AM ROOTED
ROYAL	I AM ROYAL
RECOGNISED	I AM RECOGNISED
RESILIENT	I AM RESILIENT

HOW DO YOU FEEL?

S

s

Reader says..... YOU ARE	NOW YOU SAY
SUCCESSFUL	I AM SUCCESSFUL
SPECIAL	I AM SPECIAL
SMART	I AM SMART
SIGNIFICANT	I AM SIGNIFICANT

HOW DO YOU FEEL?

T

T

Reader says..... YOU ARE	NOW YOU SAY
A TEACHER	I AM A TEACHER
TALENTED	I AM TALENTED
TREMENDOUS	I AM TREMENDOUS
TREASURED	I AM TREASURED

HOW DO YOU FEEL?

U

U

Reader says..... YOU ARE	NOW YOU SAY
UNIQUE	I AM UNIQUE
UNIVERSAL	I AM UNIVERSAL
UNDEFEATED	I AM UNDEFEATED
UNSTOPPABLE	I AN UNSTOPPABLE

HOW DO YOU FEEL?

V

V

Reader says..... YOU ARE	NOW YOU SAY
VALIDATED	I AM VALIDATED
VERSATILE	I AM VERSATILE
VICTORIOUS	I AM VICTORIOUS
VALUED	I AM VALUED

HOW DO YOU FEEL?

W

W

Reader says..... YOU ARE	NOW YOU SAY
WISE	I AM WISE
WORTHY	I AM WORTHY
WONDERFUL	I AM WONDERFUL
WORLD-CLASS	I AM WORLD-CLASS

HOW DO YOU FEEL?

X

X

Reader says..... YOU ARE	NOW YOU SAY
EXTRODIANRY	I AM EXTRAORDINARY
EXISTENCE	I AM EXISTENCE
EXTREME	I AM EXTREME
EXECUTIVE	I AM EXECUTIVE

HOW DO YOU FEEL?

Y

Y

Reader says..... YOU ARE	NOW YOU SAY
YOUNG	I AM YOUNG
YOU	I AM YOU
YOUTHFUL	I AM YOUTHFUL
YAHWEH	I AM YAHWEH

HOW DO YOU FEEL?

Z

Z

Reader says..... YOU ARE	NOW YOU SAY
ZION	I AM ZION
ZELOUS	I AM ZELOUS
ZESTFUL	I AM ZESTFUL
ZIPPY	I AM ZIPPY

HOW DO YOU FEEL?